Texas Sayings

Compiled by Anne Dingus

Great Texas Line Press
Fort Worth, Texas

Texas Sayings

For bulk sales
and wholesale inquiries
contact:
Great Texas Line Press
Post Office Box 11105
Fort Worth, TX 76110
greattexas@hotmail.com
www.greattexasline.com
817-922-8929

*To see our complete list of Texas guidebooks, humor books and
cookbooks, visit greattexasline.com*

Cover art, illustrations: Edd Patton
Cover design: Kari Crane
Editor: Amy Culbertson
Book design: Tom Johanningmeier

Printed in Fort Worth by the Swiger family of Hanson Printing

Great Texas Line Press strives to be socially responsible, donating a portion
of proceeds from several books to Habitat for Humanity of Fort Worth,
North Fort Worth Historical Society, Texas Dance Hall Preservation Inc. and
Terlingua's Big Bend Educational Foundation. Hundreds of books are donated
annually to Public Radio stations throughout Texas for fund-raising. Every
effort is made to engage Texas writers, editors, illustrators, designers and
photographers who fell victim to the newspaper industry crisis, and to
produce the books at local family-run print shops.

Introduction

Well, look what the cat dragged in: an expanded and up-dated version of my collection of Texas sayings. It's the first edition since 1996, when I published *More Texas Sayings Than You Can Shake a Stick At,* based on a hugely popular article that appeared in *Texas Monthly* magazine in 1994.

This new book, published by Fort Worth's Great Texas Line Press, contains 200 additional sayings, for a total of more than 1,600, in categories ranging from "acceptable" to "young" (with special emphasis on "crazy," "dumb," and "ugly"). This reissue contains the original illustrations by Austin artist Edd Patton as well as a new feature: "Texas Sayers." The latter is a tip of the cowboy hat to six legendary Texans whose quips we still quote: Lyndon Johnson, Ann Richards, Jim Hightower, Molly Ivins, Dan Rather and Darrell Royal.

Texas sayings are common as cornbread, old as dirt and funny as all get-out. They are unaffected, homespun expressions that link 21st-century Texans to the land we love and the history we cherish. Some sayings are instantly familiar because our parents or grandparents used them; others parallel the indisputable wisdom of biblical proverbs or *Poor Richard's Almanac*; plenty just make us laugh.

That's why millions of Texans, from farmers in one-horse

towns to lawyers in three-piece suits, still use these Texas sayings every day. They symbolize the folksy, colorful past of a state that is today sharp, shining and techno-savvy — but remembers where it came from. While country or small-town dwellers repeat them out of habit and tradition — and weather worry — urbanites are more apt to value them as folklore: a link to Texas' mythic past, to the days of the Old West, King Cotton and Big Oil.

Like blue jeans, beefsteak and prickly pear, Lone Star one-liners are a Texas constant. If you enjoy them half as much as I do, this book is for you. It's got a passel of sayings as big as all hell and half of Texas.

Anne Dingus, Austin, Texas

"If I felt any better, I'd drop my harp plumb through the cloud."

ACCEPTABLE

It's better than a poke in the eye with a sharp stick.

It don't make me no never-mind.

That's close enough for government work.

Might as well. Can't dance, never could sing, and it's too wet to plow.

Like a dead horse, I ain't kickin'.

I could sit still for that.

I could hold that in abeyance.

You can't beat that with a stick.

You can't beat that with a clawhammer.

Fair enough.

There you go.

Whatever melts your butter.

Whatever greases your wagon.

Whatever greases your griddle.

Whatever blows your skirt up.

Whatever wets your whistle.

It'll do to take along.

ADVICE

See GENERAL ADVICE.

ALL

See EVERYTHING.

ANGRY, AGGRESSIVE, ARGUMENTATIVE

She could start a fight in an empty house.

She always reckons on a ruckus.

He'd argue with a wooden Indian.

He'd argue with God Himself.

She raised hell and stuck a chunk under it.

She's the hell-raisingest woman I ever did know.

He's tearing up the pea patch.

She let me have it with both barrels.

He jumped on me like a duck on a June bug.

He was all over me like white on rice. (Can also refer to sexual advances.)

She jumped on me with all four feet.

He's got his tail up.

He's filing his teeth.

She's in a horn-tossin' mood.

She's tossin' her horns and pawin' the sod.

She's so contrary she'd float upstream.

She's dancing in the hog trough.

He'll tell you how the cow ate the cabbage. (Can also mean "straightforward.")

He'll fight with you till hell freezes over, then skate with you on the ice.

Mad as an old wet hen.

Ant-mad.

Mad as a mama cow with a sore teat.

I'm so mad I could stretch sheet iron.

I'm so mad I could eat a horny toad backwards.

I'm gonna cloud up and rain knuckles.

He's spouting steam at every joint.

She's up on her high horse. (Can also mean "arrogant" or "vain.")

Ears back, claws out.

Up on her hind legs.

I'm so mad I could stomp baby ducks.

He had a hissy fit.
He had a conniption fit.
His didy pin must be stickin' him.
He's about to blow a gasket.
He was raised on clabber and vinegar.
She got all cross-legged about it.
She's in a lather.
You wouldn't be happy if they hung you with a new rope.
That really raises my hackles.
That really burns my britches.
That burns me up like a chicken at a barbecue.
That ruffles my tail feathers.
Give' em what-for.
I'm so mad I could jump up and down and spit golden BBs.
I just about had a fit and fell back in it.
   "Fit" is likely a rhyming euphemism for a vulgar word.
That just flew all over me.
She tore up a strip about that.
He was as red as a dewberrry.
He's like a cheap gun: shoots easy but kicks hard.

ARRIVAL, GREETING
Look what the cat dragged in.
Company's comin'; add a cup of water to the soup.
We've howdied but we ain't shook.
Put on your sittin' britches.
Take your hat off, but leave your boots on.
You're a sight for sore eyes.
Let's chaw the rag.
We'll rattle before we strike.
Speak of the devil!

Hello the house!
Does your dog bite?
"Can I come in?"
Light and hitch.
The broom's behind the door.
"Quick — company's comin'!"
Cool the seat of your saddle.
I hear the thundering herd.
I'd know your hide in a tanner's shop.
I'll be there if nothing breaks or comes untwisted.
I'd know your ashes in a whirlwind.
Also see EXCLAMATIONS.

BAD, MEAN

He'd see evil in the crotch of a tree.
He'd start a fight at the drop of a hat — and he'd drop it himself.
She was born sorry.
She's as sweet as a green persimmon.
Sweet as a slop jar.
So low he'd steal the widow's ax.
So low he'd steal his mama's egg money.
So low he'd steal the flowers off his granny's grave.
So low she'd steal the nickels off a dead man's eyes.
So low he'd have to look up to see hell.
So low you couldn't put a rug under her.
So mean his mama wouldn't let him nurse.
So narrow-minded he can look through a keyhole with both eyes.
A no-account fellow.
A no-good varmint.
A low-down dirty varmint.
He's a seven-sided son-of-a-bitch.

He's a real revolving SOB.

He's a spherical SOB.

He's a son-of-a-bitch any way you look at him.

She makes a hornet look cuddly.

She'll make you pray for a pine box.

A she-bear in satin.

He looks like a sheep-killin' dog.

He wouldn't scratch his own mama's fleas.

He's got horns holding up his halo.

Tough as whiteleather. (Or "whet leather.")

"Whiteleather" refers to leather that has been specially treated to make it pliable but strong. "Whet leather" may be a variant of this or may refer to the practice of honing, or whetting, a straight razor or knife on a leather strap, or strop.

Tough as whang.

Tough as nickel steak. (Now often heard as "Tough as two-dollar steak.")

Tough as stewed skunk.

He broke bad.

Bitter as gall.

Mean as a mama wasp.

Meaner than a wounded cougar.

Meaner than a cold rattler.

Meaner than a skilletful of rattlesnakes.

Friendly as a bramble bush.

Friendly as a sticker bur.

Rough as a cob and twice as corny.

Rough as a stucco bathtub.

We're not on borrowing terms.

Enough to make a preacher cuss.

Born for Boot Hill.

Meaner than a junkyard dog.

He ain't fit to sleep with the dogs.

Hell comes for a meal wherever he hangs his hat.

She cooks razor-blade soup.

The buzzards laid him and the sun hatched him.

He had a poor upbringing.

He'd sound a sour note in a choir full of jackasses.

They turned his picture to the wall.

He was disgraced.

Two inches lower than a pregnant woman's belly.

I wouldn't let him tote guts to my pet buzzard.

I'd rather have a centipede crawl up my leg.

If I was you, I'd walk sideways to make a smaller target.

Also see DISHONEST; ANGRY; UNWELCOME.

BEAT, CONQUER, THREATEN

He gave me the wire-brush treatment.

He's suckin' heads and peelin' tails.

He'll trim your tail feathers.

He'll leave you saucered and blowed.

She ran 'em around the barn.

She put the quietus on 'em.

She jumped on me with all four feet.

She walked away with the prize persimmons.

He sandpapered me smooth.

I'll snatch you bald-headed.

I'll whip you like a red-headed stepchild.

I'll knock you plumb into next week.

I'll slap you clear into next Wednesday.

I'll hit you over the head so hard, it'll break both your ankles.

I'll knock a hole in him you can see a cat through.

He needs a double helping of whoop-ass.

I'll knock a hole in him so big you can see daylight.

I'll beat you all the way to the door of death.

I'll knock your jaw so far back you'll scratch your throat with your front teeth, if you have any.

I'm gonna cloud up and rain all over you.

I'm gonna open up a whole can of whip-ass. (Or "whoop-ass.")

He ought to be kicked to death by a jackass, and I'm just the one to do it.

He was cut and battered like a Sunday fryer.

Also see FAILURE.

BEAUTIFUL

See Pretty.

If you feel froggy,
you can just jump.
("Wanna fight?")

BIG, TALL

Fat as a boardinghouse cat.

Fat as a toad.

So big he looks like he ate his brother.

So big he has to sit down in shifts.

He hasn't seen his feet in forty years.

Big as a skinned mule and twice as ugly.

Big as Brewster County.

Big as Toad Denny.

Big as Dallas.

Big as a Brahma bull.

Big as a brisket.

Big as two cords of firewood and the ax.

Big as God.

Fat as a town dog.

Big as God's country.

Big as all hell and half of Texas.

Bigger than outside.

Big enough to walk a horse through.

Wide as two ax handles.

She's warm in winter, shady in summer.

She'd rather shake than rattle.

You don't have to shake the sheets to find her.

He'll eat anything that do.

He don't care what you call him as long as you call him to supper.

He's big enough to bear-hunt with a branch.

He's all spread out like a cold supper.

He's so tall he can't tell when his feet are cold.

Her butt looks like two hams in a tow sack.

She's built tall above her corns.

She's so tall she could fix the moon without a ladder.

Tall enough to catch ducks with a crescent wrench.

These eggs are so big it won't take many to make a dozen.

Those mosquitoes are so big they can stand flat-footed and breed
with a turkey.

Those clothes sure are sudden on him.

His pants could serve time as a pup tent.

BOASTFUL

He can strut sitting down.

He's all hat and no cattle.

He's all broth and no beans.

She's all gurgle and no guts.

She's all flash and no substance.

She uses words that go eight to a pound.

He kicks up too much dust.

He blows smoke and then says its stings his eyes.

He chamber-of-commerced it.
He's shot more buck deer in that bar than any other man in Texas.
As full of wind as a corn-eating horse.
As full of smoke as a wet-wood fire.
It takes a mighty big man to weigh a ton.
We killed a bear — Pa shot it.
  Taking undue credit.
If you get to thinking you're a person of influence, try ordering
  someone else's dog around.
She thinks she pees honey and rosewater.
Also see VAIN.

BRAVE, INTREPID

Timid as Tabasco.
Cowardly as the Comanche.
Brave as the first man who ate an oyster.
Brave as a bigamist.
Brave enough to eat at a boomtown cafe.
He's double-backboned.
He dry-holes it.
She's got more guts than you could hang on a fence.
She's full of gumption and grit.
She'd charge hell with a bucket of ice water.
She'd jump a buzz saw in her Sunday best.
She's fearful feisty.
He's got plenty of sand in his craw.
He'd shoot craps with the devil himself.
He'd fight a rattlesnake and spot him the first bite.
He knows how to die standing up.
You couldn't stop her with forty feet of rope and a snubbing post.

BUSY

He's so busy you'd think he was twins.
He's doing a land-office business.
She's jumping like water on a hot skillet.
She's got her trotting harness on.
There's no grass growing under her feet.
Busy as a one-legged man at an ass-kicking convention.
Busy as a funeral-home fan in July.
Busy as a one-eyed dog in a smokehouse.
Busy as a one-armed paperhanger.
Busy as a stump-tailed bull in fly season.
Busy as a hound in flea season.
Busy as poppin' corn.
Busy as a frog in a hot skillet.
Busy as grease on a griddle.
Busy as a sackful of tomcats.
Busy as a tick in a tar barrel.
So crowded you have to go outside to change your mind.
I'm running on one foot and kicking with the other.
I'm dealing with a passel of hassles.
I'm up to my clavicles in caca.
I got to slop the hogs, dig the well and plow the south forty before
    breakfast.
I got to get back to my rat-killing.
Blowin' and goin'.
Many fish to fry.
Many eggs to gather.
Many bodies to bury.
A lot of dirt to scratch.
Busy as a backhoe.
Busy as a quilting bee. (Or "Busy as a spelling bee.")

CAPABLE, EXPERIENCED

She's got plenty of snap in her garters.
He's got plenty of arrows in his quiver.
She's got horse sense.
She's full of mother wit.
He's got plenty of notches on his gun.
He's a right smart windmill fixer.
She keeps a weather eye out.
He knows his cans.
He could find a whisper in a whirlwind.
He knows how to cut a fat hog.
He throws a mighty wide loop.
She could swim in the air and breathe underwater.
He can lick his weight in wildcats.
He's loaded for bear. (Can also mean "drunk.")
She knows more about that than a rabbit does about running.
He don't chop up his chairs to start a fire.
He don't whittle up his kindling.
He's a three-jump cowboy.
He can ride the rough string.
If she crows, the sun comes up.
He keeps his saddle oiled and his gun greased.
She'll turn on a dime and give you nine cents change.
There's no slack in her rope.
There's no food in his beard.
This ain't my first rodeo.
Also see SMART.

CAUTION

You were too hard to raise to take chances.
Don't dig up more snakes than you can kill.

Whistle before you walk into a stranger's camp.
Don't plow too close to the cotton.
A dead snake can still bite.
A dead bee can still sting.
Don't tip over the outhouse.
Also see GENERAL ADVICE.

CELEBRATION

Let's shoot out the lights.
Let's hallelujah the county.
We'll paint the town and the water tower.
We'll go to town — or at least the far pasture.
Put the little pot in the big pot.
Throw your hat over the windmill.
He's all gussied up.
She's wearin' her Sunday-go-to-meeting clothes.
I'll be there with bells on.

CHEAP, STINGY

Tight as Dick's hatband. (Can also mean "snug" or "drunk.")
Tight as a tick. (Can also mean "drunk.")
Tight as a new clothesline.
Tight as a fiddle string.
Tight as wallpaper.
Tight as a wet boot.
Tight as a brass brassiere.
Tight enough to raise a blister.
Tighter than two coats of paint.
Tighter than bark on a log.
Tighter than the stripes on a watermelon.
He's so tight he squeaks when he walks.

He's so tight he knows all his pennies by name.

He'll squeeze a nickel till the buffalo hollers.

He'll squeeze a dollar till the eagle screams.

She has short arms and deep pockets.

She'd skin a flea for its hide.

She'll drive that car till the wheels are the size of doughnuts.

Mean as cat meat.

Not a lot of sugar for a dime.

He's so cheap that he gets out of bed to turn over so he won't wear out the sheets.

COLD

This is hog-killing weather.

There's only one strand of barbed wire between here and there, and it's down.
Said of a blizzard.

Cold as a well-digger's ass. (Often sanitized to "Cold as a well-digger's knee.")

Cold as a frosted frog.

Cold as a banker's heart.

Cold as an ex-wife's heart.

Colder than a mother-in-law's kiss.

Cold as a cast-iron commode.

Cold enough to freeze the balls off a brass monkey. (Often phrased as "Better bring in your brass monkeys.")

Cold as hell with the furnace out.

Cold as a gravestone in January.

Colder than hell on a stoker's holiday.

Cold enough to freeze ducks to the pond.

It's so cold the cows are giving milkshakes.

It's so cold I saw a dog chasing a cat, and they were both walking.

It's so cold that words are freezin'; you have to fry 'em up in
   a skillet to hear what was said.
I'm so cold I'm spittin' hailstones.
So cold I'd rather sit on an ice cube than say hello.
So cold I had to open the icebox to warm up the house.
Cold as a witch's tit.

COMMON OR COARSE
Common as pig tracks.
Common as cornbread.
Common as dirt.
Common as belly buttons.
Common as coffee grounds.
Thick as the dew on Dixie.
Thick as fleas [or burs] on a farm dog.
Thick as hops.
Baptists and Johnson grass are taking over. (Or "Breeding [or
   spreading] like Baptists and Johnson grass.")
Like a yellow cab in New York City.
Also see QUANTITY.

CONFUSED
Confused as a goat on AstroTurf.
My tongue got caught in my eyeteeth, and I couldn't see what
   I was sayin'.
I can explain it to you, but I can't understand it for you.
Cattywampus to Miss Jones'.
Seven ways to sundown.
I was so confused I couldn't tell if I'd lost my mule or found
   a rope.
Her brain threw a tie rod or two.
Also see INEPT.

CRAZY

She's a couple of sandwiches shy of a picnic.

She came right off the spool.

She stays upstairs.

> *Refers to the Southern practice of caring for a relative with mental or psychological problems at home but keeping him or her shut away from visitors, often in an upstairs bedroom.*

He's got a big hole in his screen door.

She don't know if she's a-washin' or a-hangin'.

She's one bubble off plumb.

She's one brick shy of a load.

He's a few pickles short of a barrel.

He's not playing with a full deck. (Can also mean "dishonest.")

He doesn't have both oars in the water.

She doesn't know if she's shucking or shelling.

He lost too many balls in the high weeds.

He's not firing on all four cylinders.

He's overdrawn at the memory bank.

She's got too many cobwebs in her attic.

His elevator doesn't go all the way to the top.

The porch light's on, but no one's home.

Crazy as a bullbat.

> *A reference to the common name for nighthawks and to their erratic flight patterns.*

Crazy as a bedbug.

Crazy as a betsy-bug. (Or "bess bug" or "bessie bug.")

Crazy as Larrabee's calf.

Crazy as a fundamentalist on firewater.

Goofy as a barnyard owl.

Goofy as a road lizard.

Her phone's off
the hook.

I hear you clucking, but I can't find your nest.
Wilder than an acre of snakes.
Nuttier than a squirrel's breakfast.
Her fudge didn't set.
One taco short of a combination dinner.
He's missing a wing nut or two.
He's missin' a few buttons off his shirt. And both sleeves.
Also see IMMORAL.

He's lost his vertical hold.

DARK

Dark as the inside of a wolf.
Dark as coffin air.
Dark as a pocket.
Dark as a crow.
Dark as crude.
Dark as the devil's riding boots.
Dark as truck-stop coffee.
Dark as a preacher's prediction.
Black as a blue norther.
Black as midnight in a cave in hell.
Dark as a gypsy's toenails.
Dark as outhouse dirt.

DEAD

Dead as a peeled egg.
Dead as jerky.
Dead as a doornail.
Buzzard bait.

There's a light or two burned out on his string.

The buzzards are circling.
He gave up his guitar for a harp.
She opened herself up a worm farm.
She's fertilizing the lilies of the field.
She's dead — she just won't lie down.
Her candle's been snuffed.
His picture went dark.
The devil's comin' round with his bill.
He fell off the perch.
Pretty much the trash bin for that pup.
They'll take him out in a sack.
They sent his saddle home.
He came home sideways on the saddle.
He hung up his spurs.
Flatter than a road toad.
A gone pecan.
Stone cold dead in the morning.
Dead as a wedge.
Dead as a flatiron and just as stiff.

DEPARTURE, COMPLETION
Let's light a shuck.
Let's light a rag.
Let's blow this pop stand.
Let's blow this fleapit.
Let's absquatulate.
It's time to heat up the bricks.
It's time to put the chairs in the wagon.
It's time to put the tools on the truck.
It's time to swap spit and hit the road.
It's time to put out the fire and call in the dogs.

He's heading for the wagon yard.

He turkey-tailed it for home.

Hold her, boys, she's headin' for the pea patch!

Let's go crank up the mule.

That about puts the rag on the bush.

Refers to the completion of housework, when the cleaning rag is hung outside on the nearest limb to dry.

We're off like a dirty shirt.

We're off like sour milk.

A bit of wordplay: "Off" is also used to describe foodstuffs that have begun to sour or go bad.

We're off like a jug handle.

We'uns been; you'uns come.

Got to go kill a chicken and churn. (Can also mean "busy.")

Let's take to the tall timber.

I about have all the rabbits in a corner.

Git along, little dogies.

Come see us.

Y'all come back. (Or just "Y'all come.")

Y'all hold down the fort.

The train's leavin' the station.

Church is out.

DESOLATE

It looks like hell with everyone out to lunch.

Out where the buses don't run.

Forty miles to wood, twenty miles to water, ten miles to hell.

They lived so far out in the country that the sun set between their house and town.

It's been pretty quiet out here since the buffalo died.

A gone-yonder country.

DIFFICULT, FRUSTRATING

Like trying to bag flies.

Like trying to herd cats.

Like putting socks on a rooster.

Harder than picking up sticks with your butt cheeks.

That's a long hard row to hoe.

Like tryin' to take the shine off sausage.

Like tryin' to take a drink out of a firehose.

Harder than burnin' a wet elephant. (Attributed to Darrell Royal.)

Lettin' the cat out of the bag is a whole lot easier than puttin' it
   back in.

DISHONEST, SCHEMING, UNTRUSTWORTHY

He's on a first-name basis with the bottom of the deck.

He'd steal the cross off a church.

There are a lot of nooses in his family tree.

There are liars, damn liars and politicians.

They'd rather cheat you out of it than have you give it to them
   for free.

He's crookeder than a cowbird.

He's so crooked that if he swallowed a nail he'd spit
   up a corkscrew.

She's so crooked you can't tell from her tracks if she's coming
   or going.

He's so crooked he has to unscrew his trousers at night.

He's so crooked he meets himself on the way home.

He knows more ways to take your money that a roomful
   of lawyers.

He's such a liar he'd beat you senseless and tell God you fell off
   a horse.

She lies like a tombstone.
Her promises are like pie crust — easily broken.
Don't pee on my leg and tell me it's rainin'.
He's a slant-hole driller.
He's a ring-tailed rounder.
He's a skunk-oil salesman.
Like pinto beans, she'll talk behind your back.
Lower than a mole's belly on diggin' day.
Lower than flea skis.
Crooked as a dog's hind leg.
Crooked as the Brazos.
Crooked as a barrel of fish hooks.
Greasy as fried lard.
Slicker than a slop jar.
Slicker than a boiled onion.
Slicker than a greased pig.
Slicker than deer guts on a doorknob.
Slicker than oilcloth.
Slicker than cellophane.
More twists than a pretzel factory.
I don't trust him any farther than I can throw him.
He's so two-faced his own mama nicknamed him "Iscariot."
He'd rather climb a tree to tell a lie than tell the truth
   on the ground.
Also see BAD.

DISTANCE

Down the road a piece.
A fur piece.
Turn left way past yonder.
Two hoots and a holler away.

From here to there and back again.

I won't say it's far, but I had to grease the wagon twice before I hit the main road.

I won't say it's far, but you better pack one pig and the pantry.

The sun has riz, the sun has set, and here I is, in Texas yet.

(A vintage-postcard sentiment.)

Also see LENGTH.

DRUNK, HUNGOVER

Drunkulent.

Drunk as a fiddler's bitch.

Drunk as Cooter Brown.

Drunk as a barn weasel.

Drunk as a meadow mouse.

High as the Piney Woods.

Snot-slinging drunk.

Owl-eyed and fish-gilled.

So drunk he couldn't hit the ground with his hat in three throws.

So drunk he couldn't see a hole in a ladder.

So drunk he can't scratch himself.

So drunk he can't pull his hand from his pocket.

Drunker than who shot John.

Drunker than a boiled owl.

She's been thumped over the head with Samson's jawbone.

She has a hangover.

He's got the whistlebelly thumps and skull cramps.

Don't chop any wood tonight — Daddy's comin' home with a load.

He wasn't born, just squeezed out of a bartender's rag.

He fills time with Philistines.

He's got calluses on his elbows.

He cares about nothing but Pabst and payday.
Calling for Earl (or Ralph or Ruth).
   Throwing up.
He foreswore his Fritos.
   Threw up.
He laughed at the linoleum.
   Threw up.
Jugging and jawing.
You got her drunk; you take her home.
Commode-hugging, knee-walking, falling-down drunk.
Stewed as prunes.
She's been brown-bagging it since her cradle days.
She's been lapping in the gutter again.
He's been talking to the devil and dead men.
He's got the gravel rash.
She has a guest in the attic.
Let's drown some bourbon.
We were overserved all night long.
Wall-eyed and whomper-jawed.
High as a hawk.
High as a pine.
High as a Houston prices.
Drunk as Hoogan's goat.
Store liquor has the proof on the bottle; moonshine has the proof
   in the bottle.
Also see CHEAP; IMMORAL.

DRY

Dry as a powder house.
Dry as the heart of a haystack.
The creek's so low we've started haulin' water to it.

It's been dry so long, we only got a quarter-inch of rain during Noah's flood.

So dry the fish are carrying canteens.

So dry the trees are bribing the dogs.

So dry my duck forgot how to swim.

It's so dry the birds are building their nests out of barbed wire.

So dry the Baptists are sprinkling, the Methodists are spitting and the Catholics are giving rain checks.

So dry I'm spittin' cotton.

She fainted, and it took two buckets of dust to bring her around.

So dry the fish in the stock tank got ticks. And ate 'em.

So dry the cows are givin' powdered milk.

DULL (AS A KNIFE)
It wouldn't cut melted butter.

You could scratch your back with it and never draw blood.

You might as well give it to Baby for a plaything.

You could ride all the way to Big Spring on it and never split a hair.

Like frog-giggin' with the game warden.

DULL (BORING)
As exciting as a mashed-potato sandwich.

As much fun as chopping wood.

As much fun as sitting around watching the grass grow.

As much fun as sitting around watching paint dry.

Dull as Henry's hoe.

DUMB

If a duck had his brain, it would fly north for the winter.

It he was bacon, he wouldn't even sizzle.

If all her brains were ink, she couldn't dot an "i."

If all her brains were dynamite, she couldn't blow her nose.

If he had a brain cell, it'd die of loneliness.

If dumb was dirt, he'd cover about an acre.

She was behind the door when the brains were passed out.

He carries his brains in his back pocket — when he wears pants.

She's got a single-digit IQ.

She's a little short behind the years.

She hasn't got the sense God gave little green apples.

He owns a twenty-dollar horse and a hundred-dollar saddle.

Sharp as a mashed potato.

Dumb as dirt.

Dumb as a stump.

Dumb as a box of rocks.

Dumb as a bar ditch.

Dumb as a barrel of hair.

Dumb as a wagon wheel.

Dumb as a prairie dog.

Dumb as a watermelon.

Dumb enough for twins.

He doesn't know "come here" from "sic 'em."

He doesn't know cain't from ain't.

He don't know nothing about nothing.

He don't know a widget from a whangdoodle.

He don't know diddly-squat.

If brains were leather, he couldn't saddle a flea.

He don't know pooh turkey.

She doesn't have enough sense to spit downwind.

She doesn't know enough to pound sand down a rat hole.

She doesn't know enough to keep beans out of chili.

She doesn't know any more than the man in the moon.

She doesn't know beans about it.

She don't know which end's up.

She knows as much about that than a hog does about Sunday.

He can't ride and chew at the same time.

He went to Cowpatty College.

So dumb he'd hold a fish underwater to drown it.

Her head drains faster than a bathtub.

So stupid that if you put his brains in a bumblebee, it would
    fly backwards.

So thick-headed you can hit him in the face with a tire iron and he
    won't yell till morning.

She could screw up an anvil.

He couldn't track a wagon through a mud puddle.

He couldn't find his butt with a flashlight in each hand.

He couldn't pour piss out of a boot with a hole in the toe and
    directions on the heel.

He's not the sharpest knife in the drawer.

She hasn't got a head — it's a colander with a bow on it.

Not the sharpest crayon in the box.

Grandma was slow — but *she* was old.

She don't know enough to pay attention.

Pig-simple.

He couldn't figure out a seed catalog.

He couldn't spot a black goat in a field of white sheep.

If his brain was dynamite, he couldn't blow his own hat off.

He could get lost in an acre of corn, and it winter.

His brain rattles around like a BB in a boxcar.
She couldn't find land if she was sky-diving.
Don't know a bit from a butt.
Don't know enough to sugar his tea.
Thicker than Dallas lipstick.
He rain-made you.
> *He conned you. Refers to bogus "rain-makers" who traveled the*
> *countryside telling gullible farmers and ranchers they could*
> *produce rain — for a fee — and then absconding with the money.*
He's so country that when he gets on his bike he pats its nose.
Too dumb to climb the stairs — or find his way back down.

EASY
No hill for a stepper.
Slick as a whistle.
Easy as breaking eggs.
Easy as falling off a log.
Easy as sipping cider.
Easy as picking your nose.
He's on a milk run.

EVERYTHING
The whole kit and caboodle.
The whole shootin' match.
The whole shebang.
The whole nine yards.
Everything but the kitchen sink.
Everything but the broody hen.
Everything but the hair, horns and holler.
Right down to the gnat's bristle.
Money, marbles and chalk.
Piss, pile and patty.

EXCLAMATIONS AND IDIOMS

Come hell or high water.
Lord willing and the creek don't rise.
Bless your little cotton socks!
Bless your pea-pickin' heart!
What in the Sam Hill?
Boy howdy!
Root, hog, or die!
Go like stink!
Dadgum and dagnab it!
Hell's bells!
Calf rope!
  "Enough! I surrender."
Strap it on 'em like a gas mask.
I mean to shout!
I hope to shout!
For cryin' out loud!
I don't care if it harelips the governor.
Dog me if I'll do it.
The devil and Tom Walker!
Gosh-all hemlock!
I'll be jiggered.
I'll be switched.
I'll be dipped.
I'll be go to hell.
That'll blow your skirt up.
That'll nip your wick.
That'll blow your hat in the creek.
That'll rip the rag right off of the bush.
Am I right or Amarillo?
When it gets right down to the nitty-gritty . . .

When it gets right down to the lick-log . . .
When it gets right down to the nut-cuttin' . . .
When stoop comes to grunt . . .
Well, cut off my legs and call me Shorty!
Well, eat my lunch and call me hongry!
Well, slap my mama!
Well, don't that beat all!
Well, I'll be!
Well, I swan!
Katie bar the door!
Land o' Goshen!
By the great horn spoon.
By gosh and by golly.
Also see INSULTS.

EXPENSIVE

Spendy.
Higher than a cat's back.
Higher than a city skirt.
Higher than a buzzard's hat.
As pricey as picture-show popcorn.
As dear as oysters.
Too rich for my blood.

FAILURE

She blames everything on the weather or her raising.
He got caught in his own loop.
He came close to the dollar knife.
He's just an ol' used-to-be.
She took her ducks to a poor market.
It went south.
It broke bad.

Close, but no cigar.
It fell harder than Goliath.
It fell like a milk-carton Alamo.
Also see BEAT; INEPT.

FAST

He can blow out the lamp and jump into bed before it gets dark.
He gets there in one-half less than no time.
He high-tailed it out of there.
Movin' like he was goin' for the doctor.
Quicker than hell could scorch a feather.
Quick out of the chute.
Quick as a hiccup.
Faster than small-town gossip.
Faster than a prairie fire with a tailwind.
Faster than a scalded cat.
Faster than greased lightning.
Faster than double-struck lightning.
Faster than a sneeze through a screen door.
Faster than moonshine through a tow sack.
Faster than a dust devil.
Goin' like a house afire.
Hell-bent for leather.
In a New York minute.
Like a duck on a June bug.
Like a chicken on a Cheeto.
Faster than a dose of salts.
Faster than a case of *turista*.
Faster than you can say
    howdy-do.
Lickety-split.

Any faster and she'd catch up to
yesterday.

I was outta there like a kerosened cat.
I was running like a squirrel in a cage.
He's so quick, he's even fast asleep.

FOOD, HUNGER, EATING, COOKING

Hungrier than a woodpecker with a headache.
Hungrier than a hibernating bear.
Hungrier than a bitch wolf with seventeen
    pups.

Quicker than God
could get the news.

I'm so hungry I could eat the south end of a
northbound nanny goat.
I'm so hungry I could eat a jackrabbit, ears and all.
I'm so hungry I could eat the running gears off a bull moose.
I'm having a sinking spell. (Can mean "hungry," "tired" or "faint.")
I've got the weak trembles.
    Weak and giddy from hunger; used to describe the symptoms of
    low blood sugar when blood sugar wasn't something most people
    knew about.
My belly and backbone are bumpin'.
He's wolfin' round the pot.
She fixed enough for Coxey's Army.
    Coxey's Army refers to the first major American protest march, by
    unemployed workers who were led by populist Jacob Coxey from
    Ohio to Washington, D.C., in 1894.
She rustled up some raresome grub.
It's larrupin' good.
It's soppin' good.
These hushpuppies are too good for the dogs.
Good enough to lap a lip over.
I'm full as a tick.

Full as an egg.
I'm sufferin' with comfort.
I'm feelin' peckish.
Let's surround some grub.
Tastes like stump water.
  Said of bad coffee.
Keep your fork; there's pie.
Let your vittles stop your mouth.
  "Shut up and eat."
If she'd been cooking for the North, the South would have won
  the war.
Your eyes were bigger than your stomach.
  You put more on your plate than you could eat.

FOOLISH
See INEPT.

FRIENDSHIP, ATTRACTION
The porch light is always burnin'.
Long as I got a biscuit, you got half.
He took to you like a hog to persimmons.
She took to you like sticker burs to bare feet.
Neighborly as a flea to a dog.

GENERAL ADVICE
Never sign nothing by neon.
Never call a man a liar just because he knows more than you do.
There never was a horse that couldn't be rode or a rider who
  couldn't be throwed.
Just because a chicken has wings don't mean it can fly.

36

Chicken one day, feathers the next.

Today's butcher is tomorrow's beef.

A squeaky wheel gets the grease, but a quacking duck gets shot.

A pat on the back don't cure saddle sores.

A monkey in silk is still a monkey.

A worm is the only animal that can't fall down.

A loose horse always seeks new pastures.

The wilder the colt, the finer the horse.

The wolf loses his teeth, not his nature.

Kicking never gets you nowhere, unless you're a mule.

It's better to pull your weight than to pull your gun.

It takes more to plow a field than turning it over in your mind.

It'll never show on a galloping horse.

It's better to die on your feet than to live on your knees.

You can't slop sprinklers and dippers at the same trough.

    A religious reference to differing beliefs about baptism.

You can't get lard unless you boil the hog.

You can't stomp a snake with both feet in the bucket.

You can't fry beans without lard.

If you don't like barking, throw a sop to the dogs.

If you cut your own firewood, it'll warm you twice.

If a frog had wings, he wouldn't bump his ass a-hoppin'.

If the saddle creaks, it ain't paid for.

If you lie down with dogs, you get up with fleas.

If you run with the wolves, learn how to howl.

If you can't run with the big dogs, stay on the porch.

There's never a good time to have your gun jam.

There's more than one way to skin a cat.

There's more than one way to break a dog from sucking eggs.

There's no tree but bears some fruit.

Give me the bacon without the sizzle.

Give him an inch, he'll take a mile — and you'll pay the freight.

There's a big difference between the ox and the whiffletree.

A whiffletree, also called whippletree, is the horizontal bar that connects the traces of a draft animal's harness to the load being pulled.

Pigs get fat; hogs get slaughtered.

Everyone has his own way of killing fleas.

Let bygones be bygones, but remember the Alamo. (From *Greater Tuna*.)

Don't try to teach your grandmother to suck eggs.

Don't try to teach your grandma to milk mice.

Don't toss your rope before you loop it.

Don't hang your wash on someone else's line.

Don't whistle what should be sung.

Do your Texas best.

Both men and barbed wire have their good points.

A guilty fox hunts his own hole.

Don't rile the wagonmaster.

No use winking at a pretty girl in a dark room.

Don't squat on your spurs.

Better to keep your mouth shut and seem a fool than to open it and remove all doubt.

The bigger the mouth, the better it looks when shut.

A closed mouth catches no flies.

The cowboy who straddles the fence gets a sore crotch.

Skin your own buffalo.

Clean your own catfish.

Any mule's tail can catch cockleburs.

A drought usually ends with a flood.

A lean dog runs fast.

A wink's as good as a smile to a blind mule.

The apple doesn't fall far from the tree.

Only a fool argues with a skunk, a mule or a cook.

Man is the only animal that can be skinned more than once.

With poison, one drop is enough.

He ate a bitter pill.

   He learned a hard lesson.

Even the best horse needs to be spurred once in a while.

For the man destined to become a tamale, corn shucks fall from
   heaven.

One visits the cactus only when it bears fruit.

When in Rome, write your mama.

Roosters crow; hens deliver.

If a frog had side pockets, he'd carry a handgun.

In Texas, Sundays are for churchin' and hangin'.

That's tellin' Noah about rain.

If you're gonna run with the big dogs, you can't piss like a puppy.

You got to kill a snake where you find it.

The path to the paw-paw patch don't need no signpost.

A hog can't pass a good mudhole.

Just grin and walk through the cannon smoke.

Don't jump if you can't see bottom.

Don't worry about the mule, just load the wagon.

A hit dog always howls.

If you're ridin' ahead of the herd, look back now and then to make
   sure it's still followin'.

There are ex-wives, ex-husbands and ex-Baptists, but there are no
   ex-Texans.

Like it or lump it.

The more you cry, the less you have to pee.

Never kick a cowpatty on a hot day.

If you find yourself in a hole, the first thing to do is stop diggin'.

Never slap a man who's chewin' tobacco.

There are three kinds of men: the ones who learn by readin'; the few who learn by observation; and the rest, who have to pee on the electric fence by themselves.

When the sky is blue, no one wears rose-colored glasses.

She thought she could cook — and then she sold the cow.

Critters are friendly; varmints ain't.

You don't live longer in the country — it just seems that way.

Never miss a good chance to shut up.

Pray like hell or play there.

Don't strangle yourself patting yourself on the back.

GENEROUS, CONSIDERATE

She'd give away her head if she could unfasten it.

He'd lend you his last pair of long johns.

She brings a cup of sugar every time she comes callin'.

She's mighty thoughty.

GOOD, HAPPY

So good it'll make childbirth a pleasure.

So good it'll want to make you dance naked.

Sweeter than stolen honey.

Sweeter than a baby's breath.

Sweeter than an old maid's dreams.

Happy as a clam at high tide.

Happy as a boarding-house pup.

Happy as a hog in mud.

Happy as a hog in slops.

Safe as Granny's snuff box.

Fair to middlin'.

If I felt any better, I'd drop my harp plumb through the cloud.

Clean as a coon.

Fat and sassy.

All sweetness and light.

Right mannerable.

I'm cookin' with gas.

I'm cookin' on a front burner today.

Bright-eyed and bushy-tailed.

The greatest thing since sliced bread.

The greatest thing since apple butter.

If I felt any better, I'd think it was a set-up.

My spirits rose like a corncob in a cistern.

It's back-scratchin' time at the ol' corral.

Pert as a cricket.

Fine as frog hair split four ways.

Fine as boomtown silk.

Fine as dollar cotton.

Finer than gravy on biscuits.

Finer than syrup on cornbread.

He's such a gentleman, he gets to his feet when his wife comes in with the firewood.

More fun than a packed-pew preacher.

He hung the sun, the moon, the stars and a couple of horse thieves.

He's so kind he has to hire someone to kick his dog.

I haven't had so much fun since Patton was a private.

I haven't had so much fun since Hector was a pup.

I haven't had so much fun since the hogs ate Sister.

I haven't had so much fun since the legs fell off Nell's hamster.

He's grinnin' like a pig eatin' persimmons.

He's grinnin' like a mule eatin' cockleburs.

Just as happy as if she had good sense.

Straight as a shingle.

True as a die.

She's so nice that she crosses herself when she eats devil's food cake.

She's so sweet she has sugar water in her veins.

GOODBYE
See DEPARTURE.

HANDSOME
See PRETTY.

HANDY
Handy as shirt pockets.

Handy as a rope at a hangin'.

Handy as a latch on the outhouse door.

Handy as hip pockets on a hog. (Said sarcastically.)

HAPPY
See GOOD.

HARD

Hard as a pine pew.
Hard as caliche water.
Hard as a Baptist pallet on a parlor floor.
Harder than last night's cornbread.
Harder than a banker's heart.
Also see DIFFICULT.

HELLO
See ARRIVAL.

HONEST, TRUSTWORTHY

If that ain't a fact, I'm a possum.
If I say a hen dips snuff, you can look under her wing for the can.
If I tell you a chicken can pull a plow, you can hook it up and make a crop.
You can take that to the bank.
You can bet the farm on it.
You can hang your hat on it.
He's so honest you could shoot craps with him over the phone.
He sits tall in the saddle.
He totes level.
If he says it's so, it's a calcified fact.

HOT

Hot as Hades.

Hot as a billy goat in a pepper patch.

Hot as tarnation.
Hot as the hinges of hell.
Hot as the hubs of hell.
Hot as a depot stove.
Hot as a two-dollar pistol.
Hot as a summer romance.
Hot as a pot of neckbones.
Hotter than a stolen tamale. (From Kinky Friedman.)
Hotter than whoopee in woolens.
Hotter than a preacher's knees.
Hotter than a honeymoon hotel.
Hotter than a burning stump.
Hotter than blue blazes.
Hotter than a fur coat in Marfa.
Hotter than a Dutch oven with the biscuits burnin'.
Hotter than a little red wagon. (Can also mean "successful" or
   "popular.")
Hot enough to fry eggs on the sidewalk and bacon
   on the porch.
So hot the hens are layin' hard-boiled eggs.
The heat's done addled my brain-pan.
Hotter than a Laredo parking lot.
Holler than a spadeful of fire ants.
Hotter than a whore on two-for-one day.

IMMORAL, LOOSE, WILD, PROFANE
She's just naturally horizontal.
She totes her own trailer hitch.
He was all over her like ugly on an ape.
Loose as a bucket of soot.

They call her
"radio station,"
because anyone
can pick her up,
especially at night.

He's wilder [or crazier] than a peach-orchard boar.
   *Refers to the practice of putting hogs into an orchard to eat
   the windfalls, some of which, having fermented on the ground,
   contained alcohol that would make the hogs drunk.*
He'll take up with any hound that'll hunt with him.
She'll wrap herself around you like a sweet-potato vine. (From
   Mason Williams.)
Loose as ashes in the wind.
Free as fresh air.
Free as fliers.
She don't wear much more than a ring and a smile.
He was born on the wrong side of the blanket.
They ate supper before they said grace.
They planted their crop before they built the fence.
They're hitched but not churched.
They took out a cotton-patch license.
His lips ain't no prayer book.
Do you eat with that mouth?
Do you kiss your mama with that mouth?
She's a hard dog to keep under the porch.
Too close for country dancin'.
Also see DRUNK.

INEPT, USELESS, WORTHLESS

She could fall up a tree.
He could screw up a two-car funeral.
She couldn't ride a nightmare without falling out of bed.
She couldn't count to twenty using her fingers and toes.
He couldn't knock a hole in the wind with a sackful of hammers.
She couldn't hit the floor if she fell out of bed.
He couldn't catch a cold in the Klondike.

He couldn't get a whore a date on a troop train.

He's so bad at farmin', he couldn't raise Cain.

He's such a loser he bought a suit with two pairs of pants and then burned a hole in the jacket.

She'd have to study hard to get to be a fool.

He isn't worth the bullet it would take to shoot him.

He's got no more chance than a June bug in a chicken coop.

He's worthless as wet bread.

He's worth ten dollars in Confederate money.

He doesn't know split peas from coffee.

He doesn't know gee from haw.

It looks like she sewed it with a hot needle and burnt thread.

She's like a rubber-nosed woodpecker in a petrified forest.

Snake-bit.

She's like a cow's tail — always behind.

He'd fry the skillet and throw away the handle.

She's always a day late and a dollar short.

Worthless as a pitcher of warm piss. (From Vice President John Nance Garner; the quote is often sanitized as "worthless as a pitcher of warm spit.")

Useless as two wagons in a one-horse town.

Useless as last year's bird nest.

Useless as a government employee.

Useless as ice trays in hell.

Useless as a knot in a stake rope.

Useless as ball moss.

Useless as a glass of hot gravy in July.

You might as well smoke rope.

No more good than an eyeless needle.

That doesn't amount to a hill of beans.

I need that like a tomcat needs a trousseau.

Don't just sit there like a bump on a
    log.
Like pushing a wheelbarrow with
    string handles.
Tie a quarter to that and throw it away
    and you can say you lost something.
I need that like a hog needs a sidesaddle.
Sweet-talkin' water from the well.
Not worth a zinc cent.
Useless as a right-turn signal at
    NASCAR.
Also see CONFUSED; DUMB; FAILURE.

He's Rexall.
*(He's a drugstore
cowboy.)*

INSULTS, RETORTS

Even a blind hog can find an acorn.
Even a blind chicken knows to peck the
    ground.
Anytime you happen to pass my house, I'd sure appreciate it.
Go cork your pistol.
Go sit in your highchair and throw your applesauce.
Go peddle your own produce.
Go tuck in your bib.
Were you raised in a barn?
Why shear a pig?
Mind your own biscuits.
Snap your own garters.
Thank you for that crumb.
Are you spoiled, or do you always smell that
    way?
If you think that, you've got another think
    coming.

You smell like you
want to be left
alone.

If you don't like it, you can lump it.

If you break your leg, don't come running to me.

What did you do with the money your mama gave you for singing lessons?

Even the chickens under the porch know that.

That's two different buckets of possums.

You don't sweat much for a fat girl.

Put that in your pipe and smoke it.

If you're so smart, why aren't you rich?

Cripple that horse and walk it by me again real slow.

"Repeat that slowly."

Another county heard from.

I wouldn't put him out if he was on fire.

I'll believe it when there's whales in West Texas.

Also see EXCLAMATIONS.

You couldn't carry a tune in a bucket with the lid nailed shut.

LAZY

He hangs out more often than Mama's washing.

He's like a blister — he doesn't show up until the work's all done.

He's just standing around with his teeth in his mouth.

He'll never be in danger of drowning in sweat.

She's itching for something she won't scratch for.

She's so lazy she can't even hold up her own head.

As lazy as the hound that leaned against the fence post to bark.

As lazy as a dead-man post.

Too lazy to fart solo.

Too lazy to fish.

LENGTH

Long as a rope with just one end.
Longer than a Mormon clothesline.
Longer than the way west.
Longer than a country mile.
Longer than the line at the liquor store.
Longer than Bevo's horns.
Longer than Pecos Bill.

LIAR

See DISHONEST.

LUCKY

They tried to hang him, but the rope broke.
He could draw a pat hand from a stacked deck.
He always draws the best bull.
  *A rodeo term referring to the random drawing by which bull
  riders are assigned the bulls they will compete on; the score the
  rider receives depends in part on how difficult the bull was to ride.*
He's riding a gravy train with biscuit wheels.
She could sit on the fence and the birds would feed her.
So lucky she ran around the barbed-wire fence and lightning
  missed her three times.
Also see GOOD.

MAD

See ANGRY

MEAN

See BAD.

MISCELLANEOUS FIGURES OF SPEECH

Independent as a hog on ice. (Can also mean "out of control.")

Fancier than a two-story outhouse.

Bolder than a brass spittoon.

Lively as an electric fence.

Out like Lottie's eye.
  Sound asleep or passed-out drunk.

Naked as a jaybird.

White as a motel tan.

Brown as a berry.

Purple as a possum's posterior.

Black as sin.

Black as the inside of a wolf.

Clean as a hound's tooth.

Clean as a bean in a washing machine.

Clean as a coon.
  Deftly done.

Queer as a three-dollar bill.

Slick as a gut.

Her eyes were stickin' out like the cow-catcher on a switch engine.

If it'd been a snake, it would've bit you.
  The item you were looking for was right nearby.

I don't know him from Adam's off ox. (Or Adam's housecat.)

She's still sewing for her hope chest.
  She's unmarried.

He looks like he swallowed a horse except for the tail.
  He has a beard.

I saved my manners and my muskrat.
  Said of a declined invitation.

He went off the reservation.
  He went crazy; also, he's lost.

Surprised as a pup with his first porcupine.

He's so persuasive he could tell you to go to hell and make you
   look forward to the trip.

Raised on concrete.
   Citified.

Bow-tie politics.
   A slur; the term implies bureaucracy.
Also see GENERAL ADVICE.

NERVOUS, EXCITED

Nervous as a whore in church.

Nervous as a pregnant jenny.
   A jenny is a female donkey.

Nervous as a fly in the glue jar.

Nervous as Willie waitin' at the woodshed.

Nervous as a long-tailed cat in a roomful of rockers.

Jumpy as spit [or grease] on a hot skillet.

Calm as a June bug.

Calm as a horse trough when the cavalry's passin'.

Shakin' like a cloth in the wind. (Can also mean "hungover.")

Shakin' like a mule passin' peach pits.

Running around like a chicken with its head cut off.

Bouncing around like a huckleberry on a wagon bed.

Like a wiggletail in hot ashes.

So nervous she has to thread her sewing machine, and it running.

She's chewing her bit.

He makes a pressure cooker look peaceful.

He'd worry the warts off a toad.

He won't stand hitched.

All lathered up like he's waiting for a shave.

She fell apart like a flour-sack dress.

NOISY

Noisy as two skeletons dancing on a tin roof.
Noisy as an unfed mule in a tin barn.
Noisy as white trash at a tent revival.
Noisier than cats making kittens.
Noisier than a corn-husk mattress.
Noisier than a rich girl's petticoats.
Louder than Grandpa's Sunday tie.
He learned to whisper in a whirlwind.
Dogie-loud.

OLD

Old as water.
Old as dirt.
Old as Methuselah's mama.
Old as Arbuckle's.
  A 19th-century coffee brand.
He's back on oatmeal.
Evenings are cooler than mornings.
It's been there since Hector was a pup.
He's been around since who laid the chunk.
She's been around since before water was wet.
She was around when the Dead Sea was only sick.
She's living on God's sense of humor.
His horns ain't been sawed off yet.
He's so old he keeps his own buzzards.

PATIENCE

Don't get your panties in a wad.
Don't get all het up about it.

Keep your pants [or your shirt] on.
Hot will cool if greedy will let it.
Take a tater and wait.
Wash off your warpaint.
It'll come around on the git-tar.
Also see NERVOUS; GENERAL ADVICE.

POOR

If a trip around the world cost a dollar, they wouldn't make it to
    the Oklahoma line.
Broker than the Ten Commandments.
Broker than a stick horse.
Poor as a lizard-eating cat.
Poor as church mice.
Poor as sawmill rats.
Poor as Job's turkey.
Can't make tongue and buckle meet.
She lives on the other side of across the tracks.
I ate so many armadillos when I was young, I still roll up into a
    ball when I hear a dog bark.
I'm so broke I couldn't buy hay for a nightmare.
So poor I had a tumbleweed for a pet.
So poor we had to fertilize the sills before we could raise the
    windows.
So poor we can't go window-shopping.
So poor the bank won't let me draw breath.
So poor I can't pay attention.
So poor all she has to her name is a Butterick-pattern dress.
    *Butterick is a common brand of dress pattern sold for home
    sewers.*
So poor they read the Sears catalog on Sunday.

So poor the wolf won't even stop at their door.

So poor they fry water for supper and bake it for dessert.

Too poor to paint, too proud to whitewash.

All he owns is the shirt on his bank — and the buttons are on account.

He's bent but not broke.

He's been hard-wintered.

You're liable to hear anything at their house except the jingling of change and the frying of bacon.

It's no sin to be poor — but it's damned inconvenient.

She hasn't got a pot to piss in or a window to throw it out of.

So poor he boiled the shadow of his neighbor's hog.

So poor I couldn't buy the echo off a holler.

We were a two-soup-bone family, till the dog up and drug one away.

I was so poor that if I hadn't been a boy, I wouldn't have had anything to play with at Christmas.

PREGNANT

She's got a bun in the oven.

She's sittin' on her nest.

She's got one in the chute.

She's been storked.

PRETTY, HANDSOME

I'd rather watch her walk than eat fried chicken.

She can ride any horse in my string.

She's built like a brick outhouse.

She's built like a Coke bottle and just as full of sweetness.

She cleans up real nice.

She has more curves than a barrel of snakes.

She's all dressed up like a country bride. (Or "a gambler's bride.")

He's all dressed up like a sore thumb.
She's surely ornamental.
She catches your eye like a tin roof on a sunny day.
Pretty enough to make a man plow through a stump.
So pretty you can drink her coffee anyway.
Pretty as twelve acres of pregnant red hogs.
Pretty as a red heifer in a flower bed.
Pretty as a pie supper.
Pretty as dollar cotton.
Cute as a calico kitten on down south.
Cute as a speckled pup under a red wagon.
Cute as kitten pajamas.
He's a long tall drink of water.
Handsome as a handful of spades.
You could throw her in a pond and skim off cute
   for a month.
She'd look good in a croaker sack. (Or "gunny sack"
   or "tow sack"]
Also see GOOD.

PROBLEM, TROUBLE
The cattle are getting mighty thirsty.
There's a big hole in the fence.
There are weevils in the flour sack.
That horse is heading home with an empty saddle.
I got my ox in a ditch. (From Ann Richards.)
My ox got gored.
We're up a creek without a canoe.
He's sucking for a bruise.
He loaded the wrong wagon.
He ripped his britches.

The barn door's open
and the mule's tryin'
to run.
("Your fly's down.")

I got to drain that swamp.
I got my tail in a crack.
They hung the wrong horse thief.
Time to circle the wagons.
Time to get the hell out of Dodge.
Time to paint your butt white and run with the antelope.
That's where the mule threwed Russell.
Things are going to hell in a handbasket around here.

There's a yellowjacket in the outhouse. Stickier than a taffy pull.
I ran through the woods but the bears got me.

I've got more troubles than a farmer's got oats.
Every time I have to pee, there's dishes in the sink.

QUANTITY

A passel.
A sight.
A heap.
A clutch.
A slew.
A chance.
A mess.
Umpteen.
More than you can shake a stick at.
More than Carter has pills.
More than Quaker has oats.
More than Van Camp's has beans.
Also see COMMON.

We gotta dodge that bullet.

QUIET

So quiet you could've heard a rat cough.
So quiet she heard her pantyhose run.
So quiet the dogs started barking.
Quiet as a mouse peeing on cotton.
Quiet as a Quaker meeting.
Quiet as a prairie grave.
Quiet as a noose.
As chatty as an oyster.

RARE

See SCARCE.

RICH

In tall cotton. (Or "in high cotton.")
Running with the big dogs. (Can also mean "powerful" or
    "important.")
He's one of the big-hat boys. (Can also mean "powerful" or
    "important.")
She's got more than she can say grace over.
She's got more money than a porcupine has quills.
She took rich from her mama and daddy.
Rich enough to eat her laying hens.
Rich as feedlot dirt.
Rich as Daisy Bradford.
They keep the wolves away.
He butters his bread on both sides.
They didn't come to town two to a mule.
So rich they can eat fried chicken all week long.
God gives money to the wealthy so they won't starve.

SAD, UNFORTUNATE

I feel lower than a gopher hole.
I feel so low I couldn't jump off a dime.
She eats sorrow by the spoonful.
You look like you were sent for and couldn't go.
He looks like the cheese fell off his cracker.
Sad enough to bring a tear to a glass eye.
He's the moaningfullest person I ever did see.
She wails like a new widow.
Blue as a norther.
Blue as his mama's eyes.
I'm bluer than the Panhandle sky.
Bluer than dance-hall doin's.
I've got a rare case of the mullygrubs.
I'm all cut up like a boardinghouse pie.
Jinxed as Jonah.
He got the slats kicked out from under him.
I could cry till my bones melt.

SCARCE, RARE

Scarce as hen's teeth.
Scarce as grass around a hog trough.
Scarce as rain barrels in drought season.
Rare as a fair jury.
Rare as an honest lawyer.
Rare as a poor politician.

SCARED, COWARDLY, SHY

Scared as a cat at the dog pound.
Scared as sinner in a cyclone.
He stays in the shadow of his mama's apron.

He's first cousin to Moses Rose.
A reference to an alleged coward at the Alamo.
He's yellow as mustard but without the bite.
He backed out quicker than a crawfish.
If he was melted down, he couldn't be poured
  into a fight.
She wouldn't bite a biscuit.
Yellow suits her complexion.
He's whistling past the graveyard.
He's trembling in his boots.
It scared the pudding out of me.
It scared the bejesus out of me.

He may not be a chicken, but he has his henhouse ways.

It scared the pee-
  waddin' out of me.
Shy as a crocus.
Shy as sapphires.
Shy as unshucked corn.
Whey-faced.
Lily-livered.
I feel like a possum trotted over my
  grave.

Shy as a mail-order bride.

He was so scared his eyes looked like
  two fried eggs in a lard bucket.
He couldn't scare a chicken off a nest of snakes.

SERIOUS
Serious as the business end of a .45.
Serious as polio. (Or "cancer," or "a stroke.")
Serious as an undertaker.
Serious as a TV preacher.

SHY
See SCARED.

SICK

He's got a hitch in his gitalong.
He's all stove up.
Her hopper's busted.
She looks like death warmed over.
I'm so sick I'd have to get better to die.
I feel tore down almost level to the ground.
I've got the green-apple nasties.
It ouches me something fierce.
Pitiful as a three-legged dog.
Sore as a boil.
Sore as a tenderfoot's tail.
Sick as a dog passing peach pits.
So sick he needs two beds.
Too sick to drink and too thin to plow.
As full of pains as an old window.
Green around the gills.
Blue sick.
My sawdust is leakin'.
The wheels fell off his wagon.
You're all right — you just can't do the laundry for a spell.
Just show him the castor oil. That oughta fix him.
He's one sick puppy, and we're downwind of the kennel.
My head feels like a fat lady sat on it.
Also see TIRED; DRUNK.

SLOW

He's so slow he can gain weight walking.

She's so slow she fell off the bed and didn't hit the floor until morning.
Slow as molasses. (Or "Slow as molasses in January.)
Slow as Christmas.
Slow as Grandma Moses.
Slower than Grandma Turtle.
We took the milk train.
We took the scenic route.
Slower than a congressional hearing.
Slower than a Texas drawl.

SMALL, THIN
Frying size.
Knee-high to a grasshopper.
She wears her bra backwards and it fits.
She's poor as a rail fence.
He'd have to stand up to look a rattler in the eye.
About as big as the little end of nothing.
Half as big as a minute.
No bigger than moles on a chigger.
Short as pie crust.
Not as big a bar of soap after a day's washing.
Scrawny as Ace Reid cattle.
   Ace Reid was a popular cowboy cartoonist.
Nothing but hide between the horns and the hooves.
No higher than a shirt pocket.
Thin as a bat's ear.
Thin as a gnat's whisker.
Thin as store-bought thread.
Thin as Depression soup.
Thin as a fiddle string.

Thin as a rake and twice as sexy.

Lean as a longhorn.

Lean as a lodgepole.

Flat as a fritter.

Scarce-hipped.

So skinny she has to stand up twice to make a shadow.

So skinny you could give her a Big Red and use her as a thermometer.

So skinny she shades herself under the clothesline.

So skinny his belt buckle rubbed a hole in his spine.

It's just a wide spot in the road.

   Said of a small town.

Quail-high.

They picked her before she got ripe.

   She's short.

Skinny as a garter snake.

She doesn't have enough lard in her ass to fry her ears.

SMART, KNOWLEDGEABLE

Bright as a new penny.

Smart as a hooty owl.

Smart as a whip.

She's got a mind like a steel trap.

She's a walking encyclopedia.

He's deep as the Piney Woods.

He's deep as a slough.

There's no flies on my mama.

Sharper than a pocketful of toothpicks.

It don't take him long to look at a horseshoe.

He's got bobcat logic.

Wise as a treeful of owls.

She reads so much they had her tested for bookworm.
He's all over that like hair on a grizzly.
He's all over that like syrup on biscuits.
Also see CAPABLE.

SOFT

Soft [or smooth] as silk [or satin].
Soft as a two-minute egg.
Soft as a calf's ear.
Soft as a señorita's skin.
Soft as blackstrap molasses.
Soft as rainwater.
Soft as ginned cotton.

STRONG

His breath's so strong you could hang out the wash on it.
His breath's so strong it could light the stove.
Strong as acky-forty.

A reference to aqua fortis, an old-fashioned term for nitric acid, a corrosive solution used in refining ore and to stain wood.

Strong as an ox.
Strong as Samson.
Stronger than moonshine.
Stronger than a garlic milkshake.
Horse-tall, hog-strong, bull-stout.
That coffee's so strong it'll put hair on your chest.

That coffee's so strong it'll walk into your cup.

That coffee's so strong it'll raise a blood blister on a boot.

So strong he makes Samson look sensitive.
So strong he could make a Texas Ranger cry.
Strong as a bachelor's socks.

STUBBORN, PERSISTENT

Stubborn as a splinter.
Stubborn as a scar.
Hame-headed.
   A hame is one of the two curved pieces of a harness that fits
   around the animal's neck.
Stubborn as mesquite.
Stubborn as a mule in clover.
He'll stick to it like an East Texas chigger.
She stuck to it like a June bug to a screen door.
He's deaf in one ear and won't hear out of the other.
She's got no more reason than a stone.
Stubborn as crabgrass.

STUPID

See DUMB.

TALKATIVE, PERSUASIVE

She could talk a coon right out
   of a tree.
He could talk the legs off a
   chair.
He could talk the gate off its
   hinges.
He could talk the hide off a
   cow.

She speaks ten words a
second, with gusts to fifty.

She could talk the ears off a mule.

She could talk the horns off a billy goat.

He shoots his mouth off so much he must eat bullets for breakfast.

He's got a ten-gallon mouth.

She's a dry-hole gusher.

Her tongue is plumb tuckered.

She's got tongue enough for ten rows of teeth.

He blew in on his own wind.

His brain don't work if his mouth ain't movin'.

Making chin music.

Making his teeth rattle.

She has a bell clapper instead of a tongue.

He was vaccinated with a Victrola needle.

She talks so much that when she dies they'll have to take a stick
and beat her tongue to death.

He's harvesting a bumper crop of bullshit.

A dog that leaves a bone takes one too. (Said of a gossip.)

Pour the tea!

"Tell me the details!"

If you can't stop squeaking, carry your own oil can.

He could talk a cat off a fish cart.

THIN
See SMALL.

TIGHT
See CHEAP; DRUNK.

TIME
Longer than a month of Sundays.

Longer than a wet week.

Longer than a backslider's sermon.
From can't see to can't see. (Or "From "can to can't.")
From hell to breakfast.
I spent a year there one day.
They've been married so long they're on their third bottle of
    Tabasco.
Also see OLD.

TIRED

She looks like she been chewed up, spit out and stepped on. (Can
    also mean "ugly.")
She looks like she was rode hard and put away wet. (Or "... rode
    hard and put up wet.")
She looks like chewed twine.
He looks like Bowser's bone.
His eyes look like two burn holes in a mattress.
Her eyes look like cherries in the snow. (Can also mean "drunk"
    or "hungover.")
Her eyes look like tomatoes in a glass of buttermilk. (Can also
    mean "drunk" or "hungover.")
He's panting like a lizard on a hot rock.
She's plumb tuckered out.
I'm more wore out than a flour-sack dress.
I was born tired and I've since suffered a relapse.
I'm holding myself together with both hands.
I'm near about past going.
I'm so tired I knocked a hole in my chest with my chin.
I'm so tired I could sleep on a barbed-wire fence.
I feel like the tail end of pea time.
My tongue's hanging out a foot and forty inches.

My dogs are barkin'.
One wheel down and the axle draggin'.
Tired as a boomtown whore.

TROUBLE
See PROBLEM.

TRUTHFUL
See HONEST.

UGLY
She's so ugly she'd make a freight train take a dirt road.
She's so ugly she'd curdle the soup.
He's so ugly he's scare the maggots off a gut wagon.
He's so ugly his cooties
   have to close their eyes.
He looks like he was shot
   out of a cannon and
   missed the net.
He looks like the dogs have
   been keepin' him under
   the porch.
She looks like she was born
   downwind of the
   outhouse.
She looks like she fell face-
   down in the sticker patch
   and the cows ran over
   her.
Wall-eyed as a frog.

So ugly she has to sneak up on a glass
of water.

He looks like he was dragged through hell backwards and beat with buzzard guts.

So ugly the tide wouldn't take her out.

So ugly his mama had to tie a pork chop around his neck so the dogs would play with him.

So ugly his mama takes him everywhere she goes so she doesn't have to kiss him goodbye.

So ugly only his mama loves him — and she waits till payday.

So ugly his mama wore blinders when he nursed.

So ugly she has to slap her feet to make them go to bed with her.

So ugly that when he was born the doctor slapped his mama.

So ugly his face would stop an eight-day clock.

So ugly he could hold up a five-day rain.

So ugly that when he died, folks asked, "How could they tell?"

He got whipped with an ugly stick.

He fell into the River Stinx.

His mama had more hair in the mole on her chin.

He looks like he was pulled through a knothole backwards.

She looks like ten miles of bad road.

He looks like he sorts bobcats for a living.

She's so buck-toothed she could eat corn through a picket fence.

He's so bow-legged he couldn't catch a pig in a ditch.

He's so cross-eyed he can stand up in the middle of the week and see two Sundays.

He's so freckled he looks like he swallowed a quarter and broke out in pennies.

Freckled as a guinea egg.

Jimmy-jawed as a bulldog.

Hog-ugly.

Ugly as a mud fence.

Ugly as homemade soap.

Ugly as homemade sin.
Ugly as Grandpa's toenails.
He's got a face like the back
  end of bad luck.
She can't help being ugly —
  but she could stay home.
He couldn't get a date at
  the Chicken Ranch with a
  truckload of fryers.
  The Chicken Ranch was a
  legendary brothel near La
  Grange on which the musical
  and movie The Best Little
  Whorehouse in Texas *was*
  based.

I wouldn't take her to a dog
  show even if she had a chance
  of winning.

He looks like he was inside the
outhouse when the lightning struck.

If I've got to have me a mole, I
  want a nice long hair right in the middle of it.
I look like the wrath of God.
He's got lovin' eyes — they're always looking at one another.
Her teeth are like the stars — they come out at night.
She's got skin like cream and a face like clabber.
She could bite through bacon without greasing a gum.
She's got a face long enough to eat oats out of a churn.
He's got a great face for radio.
She's got a face like an unmade bed.
His dance card is always empty.
She's so cross-eyed, when she cries the tears run down her back.
She's so ugly, a rat wouldn't kiss her if she had cheese in her teeth.

He looks like a basted turkey.
She pulled off her Halloween mask and the kids all screamed.
Uglier than a bowling shoe.

UNACCEPTABLE

Not what I had my face fixed for.
Like hugging a rose bush.
Nothing to write home about.
That dog won't hunt.
That really sticks in my craw.
I'd just as soon bite a bug.
I'd rather pick cockleburs out of a skunk's rear end.
I'd rather be covered with honey and staked out over an ant bed.
I'd rather chew tinfoil.
I'd rather roughhouse with a Texas Ranger.
I'd rather run over a skunk.
I'd rather slide down a banister of razors into a tub of alcohol.
I'd rather sleep on sandpaper.
I'd rather eat peas without pork.
I wouldn't have him if his head was strung with gold.
I don't cotton to it.
Step on it before it starts crawling.
Also see FAILURE.

UNSOPHISTICATED

She just fell off the turnip truck. (Or "the tater truck," "the
  watermelon truck" and so on.)
He's so country he thinks a seven-course meal is a six-pack and a
  possum.
I've been to two county fairs and a goat-ropin', and I ain't never
  seen nothing like it.

He's crude as new oil.
She's country as cow chips.

UNWELCOME

As welcome as an egg-sucking dog.
As welcome as an outhouse breeze.
As welcome as a screwworm and his sisters.
As welcome as a skunk at a lawn party.
As welcome as a tarantula at a tea party.
As welcome as a wet shoe.
As welcome as a tornado on a trail drive.
As welcome as a train wreck.
As welcome as cold hands on a milk cow's udder.
As welcome as a drunk at a revival.
As popular as a frog in the guacamole.
As popular as a porcupine at a nudist colony.
Also see BAD.

USELESS

See INEPT; WASTING TIME

VAIN

He broke his arm patting himself
   on the back.
He's struttin' his okra.
   Showing off.
She sure is biggety.
I'd like to buy him for what's he
   worth and sell him for what
   he thinks he'd bring.

He thinks the sun comes up just
to hear him crow.

She's so spoiled salt couldn't save her.
She's got more airs than an Episcopalian.
If she gets to heaven, she'll ask to see the upstairs.
I wish I'd been born rich instead of so darned good-looking.
Also see BOASTFUL.

WARNING
See CAUTION.

WASTING TIME
Preaching to the choir.
  Trying to convince someone who already shares your opinion.
Just ratting around.
Burning daylight.
Beating the devil around the stump.
Burning green wood for kindling.
Arguing with a wooden Indian.
Arguing with a marble statue.
Closing the barn door after the mule is out.
Whistling up the wind.
Pissing up a rope.
Hollering down a well.
Hollering down a rain barrel.
Fadoodling.
He's soap-tracked.
  Spinning his wheels.
He's bailing out his boat with a spoon.
She's chasing a hawk's shadow.
The more you run over a possum, the flatter it gets.
Also see LAZY; INEPT.

WEAK

Weak as well water.
Weak as Yankee chili.
Limp as a lap-baby.
That man's so weak a two-year-old could tump him over.
That's coffee's so weak I had to help it out of the pot.

WEALTHY

See RICH.

WEATHER

So foggy the birds are walking.
Looks like it's going to clabber up and rain.
So dusty the rabbits are digging holes six feet in the air.
Panhandle rain.
  A dust storm.
The wind's blowing like perfume through a prom.
It's so windy the thermometer's plumb horizontal.
It's blowing so hard we're using a log chain instead of a wind
  sock.
It's so windy it blew the latch right off the door.
It's right airish out.
It's fixin' to come on.
Windier than a fifty-pound bag of whistling lips.
Windier than a Baptist preacher on Rally Day.
Nice night for a tornado.
Texas has four season: drought, flood, blizzard and twister.
A real gully-washer.
A real toad-strangler.
The devil's beatin' his wife with a fryin' pan.
  Said of simultaneous rain and sunshine.

The mesquites ain't out yet.
  "It's too early in the year." Refers to the fact that mesquites are among the last trees to leaf out in the spring.
Wet enough to bog a saddle blanket.
It rained so hard it filled up the egg basket.
I'm not sayin' it rained hard, but folks took shelter two by two.
It rained a barbed-wire fence plumb in two.
So windy it blew the mustard right off my hot dog.
Also see HOT; COLD; DRY.

WILD
See CRAZY; IMMORAL

WISE
See CAPABLE; SMART.

WORTHLESS
See INEPT; WASTING TIME.

YOUNG
Full of piss and vinegar.
  Often sanitized as "Full of sass and vinegar."
Green as guacamole.
Green as a gourd.
Green as fresh firewood.
He hasn't shed his first skin.
He's somewhere between grass and hay.
He's climbing up fool's hill.
He's wet behind the ears, 'cause his mama gave him a bath last night.

"That's all she wrote!"

Texas Sayers

Lyndon Johnson

Lyndon Baines Johnson (1908-1973) was raised on a ranch in the Texas Hill Country and went on to become the 36th president of the United States.

"Being president is like being a jackass in a hailstorm. There's nothing to do but stand there and take it."

"Every man has a right to a Saturday night bath."

"In our house there was always prayer — aloud, proud and unapologetic."

On his detractors: "Better to have 'em inside the tent pissin' out than outside the tent pissin' in."

On a fellow politician: "I hope his mind isn't as empty as his desk."

In a letter to his tailor, on why certain new pants were uncomfortable: "It's just like riding a wire fence."

"Only two things are necessary to keep one's wife happy. One is to let her think she is having her own way, and the other is to let her have it."

"You aren't learning anything when you're talking."

"In politics you have to learn that, overnight, chicken shit can become chicken salad."

"While you're saving your face, you're losing your ass."

Ann Richards

Ann Richards (1933-2006), the 45th governor of Texas, was famous for her folksy, off-the-cuff wit.

"I got my ox in a ditch."

"In politics your enemies can't hurt you, but your friends can kill you."

"I am the only child of a very rough-talking father. So don't be embarrassed about your language. I've either heard it or I can top it."

"I get a lot of cracks about my hair, mostly from men who don't have any."

"The higher the hair, the closer to God."

"I've been tested by fire, and fire lost."

"My daddy used to tell me I could do anything. I was in college before I found out he might be wrong."

"You can put lipstick and earrings on a hog and call it Monique, but it's still a hog."

On her solidarity with stay-at-home moms: "Let me tell you, sisters — seeing dried egg on a plate in the morning is a lot dirtier than anything I have encountered in politics."

When asked what she would have done differently, if she had known she'd be a one-term governor: "I would probably have raised more hell."

Jim Hightower

Jim Hightower (1943-) served as Texas' commissioner of agriculture from 1983 to 1991 and remains a popular Democratic pundit.

"He was a toothache of a man."

"Even the smallest dog can lift its leg on the tallest building."

"You can still make a small fortune in agriculture. Problem is, you have to start with a large one."

"He's bi-ignorant."

"The opposite of courage is not cowardice — it is conformity. Even a dead fish can go with the flow."

"My mother used to tell me that three wrongs don't make a right. But I soon discovered that three left turns do."

"The only difference between a pigeon and the American farmer today is that a pigeon can still make a deposit on a John Deere."

"Here come the Democrats again, just weaker than Canadian hot sauce."

"There's nothing in the middle of the road but a yellow stripe and dead armadillos."

"It's hard for the donkeys to win the race if they're carrying the elephants on their backs."

"The Bible says that on the sixth day God created man. Right then and there, God should have demanded a damage deposit."

"The water won't clear up until we get the hogs out of the creek."

Dan Rather

Dan Rather (1931-), one of America's best-known journalists, was anchor for the CBS Evening News *for 24 years.*

"Always marry a woman from Texas. No matter how tough things get, she's seen worse."

"To err is human, but to really foul up requires a computer."

"Don't taunt the alligator till after you've crossed the creek."

"I'd much rather wear out than rust out."

"This race is closer than Lassie and Timmy."

"This race is hotter than a Times Square Rolex."

"This race is hotter than the devil's anvil."

"This race is humming along like Ray Charles."

"The presidential race is swinging like Count Basie."

"I'm proud to say I've never been anyone's lap dog."

"And now the sequence of events, in no particular order."

"An intellectual snob is someone who can listen to the William Tell Overture and not think of the Lone Ranger."

"Once the herd starts moving in one direction, it's very hard to turn."

"I'd rather walk through a fire in a gasoline suit."

"If I didn't have a front-row seat on history, at least it was a seat on the aisle."

"If a frog had side pockets, he'd carry a handgun."

"His lead is as thin as turnip soup."

"His lead is as thin as November ice."

"This situation in Ohio would give an aspirin a headache."

"He is sweeping through the South like a big wheel through a cotton field."

On a losing candidate: "He's got his back to the wall, his shirttails are on fire and the bill collector's at the door."F

Molly Ivins

Molly Ivins (1944-2007) was a beloved humorist and columnist, a dedicated liberal and a longtime observer of politics in Texas.

"As they say around the Texas Legislature, if you can't drink their whiskey, screw their women, take their money and vote against 'em anyway, you don't belong in office."

"Good thing we've still got politics in Texas. Finest form of free entertainment ever invented."

"I dearly love the state of Texas but consider that a harmless perversion on my part and discuss it only with consenting adults."

"Being slightly paranoid is like being slightly pregnant — it tends to get worse."

"I've always been an optimist. It's practically a congenital disorder with me."

"I believe in practicing prudence at least once every two or three years."

On Bill Clinton: "Weaker than bus station chili."

"The thing is this: You got to have fun while you're fightin' for freedom, 'cause you don't always win."

"Sometimes I'd feel better with Punxsatawney Phil in the Oval Office. At least he doesn't lie about the weather."

"Polarizing people is a good way to win an election and also a good way to ruin a country."

"I don't mind so much that newspapers are dying. It's watching them commit suicide that pisses me off."

"People at the top of the heap have a hard time even seeing those on the bottom. They practically need a telescope."

On George W. Bush: "He's quite a fast learner. When you approve of a politician, this is called flexibility; when you don't, it's called lack of principle."

"All anyone needs to enjoy the state legislature is a strong stomach and a complete insensitivity to the needs of the people."

Darrell Royal

Darrell K. Royal (1924-2012) was head football coach at the University of Texas at Austin from 1957-1976, during which time the Longhorns won three national championships and eleven Southwest Conference titles.

"Dance with the one who brung ya."

"They cut us up like boardinghouse pie. And that's real small pieces."

"Three things can happen when you pass, and two of them are bad."

"If worms carried pistols, birds wouldn't eat 'em."

"You got to think lucky. If you fall in a mudhole, check your back pocket. You might have caught a fish."

"All the white meat is gone. There's nothing but necks left on the platter."

"Every coach likes those players who, like trained pigs, will grin and jump right in the slop."

"Breaks balance out. The sun don't shine on the same ol' dog's rear end every day."

"Ol' ugly is better than ol' nuthin'."

"They're like a bunch of cockroaches. It's not what they eat and tote off, it's what they fall into and mess up that hurts."

"You don't have to explain victory, and you can't explain defeat."

"I was so poor I had a tumbleweed as a pet."

"I was as nervous as a pig in a packing plant."

"He runs like a bucketful of minnows."

"He could run like small-town gossip."

"He's quick as a hiccup."

"He's smoother than smoke through a keyhole."

"He doesn't have a lot of speed, but maybe Elizabeth Taylor can't sing."

"Winning coaches must treat mistakes like a copperhead in the bedclothes."

"I had hoped God would be neutral."

"I never have planned a lot of future. It's one day at a time."

Index